Grandfather's Old Bruk-a-Down Car

Grandfather's Old Bruk-a-Down Car

John Agard

Illustrations by
Kevin Dean

RED FOX

A Red Fox Book

Published by Random House Children's Books
20 Vauxhall Bridge Road, London SW1V 2SA

A division of Random House UK Ltd
London Melbourne Sydney Auckland
Johannesburg and agencies throughout the world

Copyright © text John Agard 1994
Copyright © illustrations Kevin Dean 1994

1 3 5 7 9 10 8 6 4 2

First published in Great Britain by
The Bodley Head Children's Books 1994

Red Fox edition 1997

Printed and bound in Great Britain by
Cox & Wyman Ltd, Reading, Berkshire

Papers used by Random House UK Limited
are natural, recyclable products made from wood grown in
sustainable forests. The manufacturing processes conform to
the environmental regulations of the country of origin.

RANDOM HOUSE UK Limited Reg. No. 954009

ISBN 0 09 930140 7

For Father Stanley Maxwell, my 'O'-level English teacher, Saint Stanislaws College, Georgetown, Guyana. To us he was Maxy, who said Mass very quickly; assembled a transistor radio inside a soap dish; and most of all made words and the dictionary fun.

CONTENTS

MY STAMP ALBUM

My stamp album
is a window
to the world.
Little squares
of blues
and blacks
and reds
and whites
and yellows
and greens
and pinks too.

Well, then, suppose
I say to you
my stamp album
is a window
full of windows.

Which one do you want
to look through?

But first, let's pretend
your eyes
are curtains.

MA FLO'S ROCKING CHAIR

When you pay us a visit
   you can sit anywhere
but mind you don't sit
   in Ma Flo's rocking chair.

You can make yourself snug
   on the patchy-patchy rug
You can let your limbs sag
   in the squashy bean bag.

You can cock up your feet
   on the chair with cane seat
You can stretch out on the sofa
   like a regular loafer.

You can sit there looking cool
   on the three-legged stool
You can make yourself at home anywhere
   except in Ma Flo's rocking chair.

When Ma Flo was alive
   she always sat there
reading her Bible, combing her hair,
   or simply gazing with a faraway stare.

Then one day out of the blue
   she whispered in our ear:
'All-you young people think ghosts aren't real
   but I'll haunt all who warm their tail

   in this rocking chair . . .'

GUESS MY WHISTLE

It's not one of plastic
It's not one of tin
But when I blow it
It makes quite a din.

It's not one you can lose
It's not one you can win
It's made of my mouth
Two fingers and wind.

SISTER ROSE'S TAMBOURINE

She shakes it wicked
   She shakes it mean
She puts her soul
   in that tambourine.

Sends a tremoring
   all the way to your toes –
that famous tambourine
   belonging to Sister Rose.

Takes you down
   to the valley
of the shadow
   where the dead would go.

Takes you up
   to heaven's gate
where the angels wait
   in a golden glow.

Give thanks for hands
Give thanks for sound
Give thanks for the tambourine
that makes Sister Rose a queen.

MR RUCKET'S BUCKET

Mr Rucket had a bucket
which he never ever lent
for fear it might receive a dent.

Then again, you could never tell,
thought Mr Rucket.
Some fool might chuck it down the well.

When news spread that Mr Rucket was dead
all the people in the village said:
'He sure gone with he bucket to hell'.

What a surprise it was to find
Mr Rucket's bucket full of coins inside,
and a little note that read:

'This is to buy a new church bell'.

MY BALL

My ball is a bouncing sun
that lights up the park.

When I take my ball to bed
it's my shining moon in the dark.

No one believes me when I tell them
that my ball catches me instead.

20

MUM'S TYPEWRITER

Mum is a wizard
on a typewriter.
An absolute ace.
There's one she keeps
in an old grey case.
Letters come out by leaps
on to the page
until rows of words
go marching by neat-neat.

Mum is a tapdancer
on typewriter keys
but she uses fingers
instead of her feet.
Sometimes she lets me
have a go.
But I'm not so quick.
One thing I know though,
she won't swop
her old manual
for a new electric.

My Mum gives her typewriter
a little hug
and says: 'This old faithful
will never need a plug'.

GRANDFATHER'S OLD
BRUK-A-DOWN CAR

It does make a lot of smoke
and people like to joke
about my grandfather's old bruk-a-down car.

It can only run slow
but it still can go
my grandfather's old bruk-a-down car.

It mightn't go fast
but it can still travel far
my grandfather's old bruk-a-down car.

It does make a racket
every time he try to start it
my grandfather's old bruk-a-down car.

He does have to crank it and crank it
and when at last the engine rev-up
he does thank it and thank it.

People would tease him by calling
his old bruk-a-down car 'SCRAP-IRON'
but my grandfather calls it 'MY STALLION'.

MY CAMERA

My camera
catches movement
slow or quick

My camera
has a shutter
but doesn't click

My camera
points to the ground
and takes out the sky

My camera
needs no film
but is a spy

My camera
(have you guessed?)
is my eye.

AUNTIE NELL'S GRIP

Auntie Nell got a suitcase. She calls it her gr
Auntie Nell is forever going on some trip.

She been overland. She been oversea.
That suitcase seen more places than you or m

She's always knocking on some relative's door
Once, without warning, she showed up in
Singapor

The day she left her born-island Tobago
She said: 'Wherever I go, this grip got to go'.

Whenever she's not travelling all over the glo
Auntie Nell keeps her suitcase on top her
wardrob

With a leather belt she'll strap it extra tight.
Then soon she and her grip are off on a flight

The truth is Auntie Nell is scared of flying.
But she feels that lucky grip will keep her fro
dyin

26

THE GIANT'S SPECTACLES

His spectacles are two huge moons
on the tip of his nose.

The frame was made from the shell
of the rarest of armadillos.

The lens formed from finest glass
sent in from the isle of crystal.

The screws are definitely golden.
The giant would not settle for brass.

But he's glaring
       staring
       peering
       leering

with a giant's unfathomable eye
till a tiny marble of a tear
falls on the rim of his spectacles.

But why has the giant begun to cry?

He thinks it's not fair
that a giant with such fantastic glasses
can neither read nor write.

But at least none in the world can beat him
for glaring
    staring
    peering
    leering
over that marvellous rim.

MY CHAIR

My chair
is not square.
It's sort of round.

My chair
can be on
or off the ground.

My chair
comes with me
when I go to town.

My chair
gives my feet a rest
and my feet
give my chair a rest.

My chair
(have you guessed?)
is my bum.

THE POET'S PEN

I'm a hunter with a pen
and I'm tracking down words.

Some stay high as birds
Some keep low as worms.

But I'm armed with my pen
and I'll track words to their den.

Some words are snakes
I hear their hiss.

Some words are tigers
I hear their roar.

Some words are scorpions
Watch out for their sting.

But I'm hiding with my pen
and I'll catch them in a wink.

My God, I've run out of ink!

GRAMMA'S BISCUIT TIN

Gramma's biscuit tin
beside her bed
has odds and ends
like covers
that once belonged to pens
and letters
from old-old friends.

Gramma's biscuit tin
beside her bed
has bits and pieces
like keys
that once belonged to locks
and screws
from broken clocks.

Gramma's biscuit tin
beside her bed
has all sorts of things
like rings
that once belonged to curtains
and fuses
from forgotten plugs.

And Gramma uses
that biscuit tin
beside her bed
for keeping her bingo card.
She prays to the Lord
that one day she'll win.
But win or lose
her dreams are in
that biscuit tin.

THE SPELLER'S BAG

Here a bone.
Here a stone.
In my bag
I keep them all.

A stone brought me
by the sea.
A bone taken from where
I'll never tell thee.

A bone, a stone,
a feather, a shell,
all in my bag
to cast a spell.

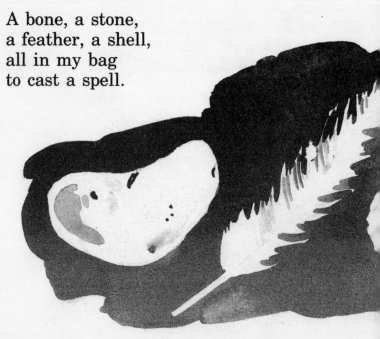

A shell that taught
the wind to howl.
A feather stolen
from the back of an owl.

Then again it might be
from a raven's neck.
I'll never tell thee.

Look inside all who dare.

Inside my bag
you'll find your fear.

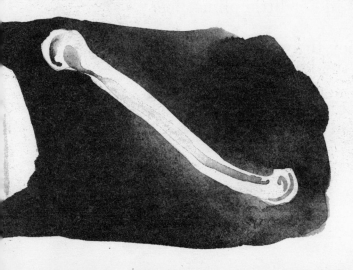

HEFFIE'S LITTLE PLIMSOLLS

She leapt over fields
She stepped over stones
all in her little plimsolls.

She followed birdcalls
She dared waterfalls
all in her little plimsolls

On top of grassy hills
She gambolled she rolled
all in her little plimsolls.

She played among the pebbles
She strayed among the bluebells
all in her little plimsolls.

They thought she was under the spell
of the fairies and the trolls

Heffie simply said she had grown
tired of her Lego and her dolls.

BRIDGET'S LITTLE GREEN BOTTLE

Bridget keeps
a little green bottle
on her window sill
close to where she sleeps
and inside that green bottle
a little man leaps.

How he got there
nobody knows
and it's not our business to ask.
But I suppose
that little green bottle
has an interesting past.

Where she got it from
Bridget will not tell,
but when midnight creeps
on her window sill
and the moon has cast
its yellow spell,
that's when the little man
in the green bottle leaps.
Yes, when the whole world sleeps
he leaps, he leaps, he leaps.
And that's when Bridget peeps.

MAN WITH THE HAT

I keep on
my hat
whatever I do

In the house
on the street
in the bath
in the loo

I keep on
my hat
whatever I do

Running
walking
eating
working

I keep on
my hat
whatever I do

Even at night
when I sleep
I keep on
my hat
to stop
my dreams
slipping through

MY WELLIES

They've splashed
up puddles

They've mashed
up mud

They've skipped
on leaves

They've tripped
on roots

They've hopped
with grasshoppers

And I wouldn't swop
them for anything

Not these old smelly wellies
that once belonged to a garden gnome.

44

AUNTY FRAN AND HER FAN

With a wave of her hand
Aunty Fran flutters her fan
and feathers unfold
in a peacock-style.

Sometimes she'd smile
and say, 'Life ain't what it used to be.
Do you know in days of old
I was a theatre lady?
This fan takes me back to distant lands
and all the people I have been.
All it takes is a flutter of a fan
for your dear Aunty Fran
to be an African queen
or a princess of Japan.'

Aunty Fran, wherever you are,
I think I know now what you mean.
And when I'm feeling lonely
I simply unfold your fan
and a thousand faces unfold for me.

GRANDMOTHER'S WAR-CORSET

Blazing and battle-set
Who can forget
       the sight
of my grandmother in her war-corset?

Let armies come by day
Let armies come by night
       their war-gear
       will not scare
my grandmother in her war-corset.

Let them put on their bullet-proof vests
Let them put on their shirts of steel
       Sound the bugle in the east
       Roll the drum in the west
my grandmother will meet them in her war-
                   corset.

No charging horse she rides
No glinting sword she carries
        But when the battle-rain descends
        And the bird of death leaves its
nest
my grandmother will be waiting in her
                        war-corset.

For believe me, that war-corset
        was woven by the hand of wind
        was sewn with lightning's thread
        was dipped in night's cauldron
And held tight by thunder's buckle.

49

MY CRAYON

Do you know
with this stump
of a crayon
I can make a rainbow
grow out
of your mouth
and do a tree
like a green mop
where your neck ought to be?

Do you know
with this stump
of a crayon
I can give you
two bananas for ears
and wriggly worms
for your hair
and have blue tears
falling from the bees
of your eyes?

Do you know
with this stump
of a crayon
I can if I wish
make your nose spade-shape
your face a dish
and put two bright leaves
where your eyebrows
ought to be?

You don't believe me?
Well, just pass me
my incredible
indelible crayon.

PAPA JOE'S VIOLIN

When you hear a song climbing up the hill
till the oldest bones feel a thrill –
that could only be Papa Joe's violin

When you hear a breeze blowing through
                                    strings
you know it must be Papa Joe's violin –
with its old strapped up bow

What makes it so special, nobody seems to
                                    know.
But some say under a full-moon glow
close to the spreading silk-cotton tree

52

There the devil once fingered that violin
and filled it with heavenly melody.
But Papa Joe had to promise one thing –

He must willingly play for the devil's wedding.

Whenever people tell that story
Papa Joe would simply wink with a golden
                                        grin
and say, 'Who believe that, would believe
                                        anything'.

MY UMBRELLA

When it's raining my umbrella keeps me dry
although the winds always try to take it high.

Otherwise my umbrella sits in the corner
like a bird that has forgotten how to fly.

54

UNCLE NEDD'S ALARM CLOCK

He doesn't keep it near his bed
to invade his dreaming head.

It doesn't make a ringing sound
to disturb his slumberdown.

It hasn't got a night-time glow
within sight of his pillow.

Oh no, says Uncle Nedd, twinkling his eyes.
I have a secret clock which helps me to rise.

It's a little cuckoo that never fails
and it sits among the branches of my brain.

I simply tell myself what time I'd like to wake
and my internal cuckoo gives me a shake.

COUSIN BOBO'S BATEAU

Down the mighty River Orinoco
Cousin Bobo in he little bateau
Paddle in hand and he row-row-row

Tide high tide low rapid water flow
Cousin Bobo in he little bateau
Paddle in hand and he row-row-row

Bad wind blow full-moon glow
Cousin Bobo in he little bateau
Paddle in hand and he row-row-row

He ain't afraid the mighty Orinoco
He ain't afraid piranha bite he toe
He ain't afraid mermaid pull he low

Not when he in that little bateau
which he christened THE SHADOW –
a boat that born to float
on the roughest-roughest billow.

'When my time to go', says cousin Bobo,
'Tell them bury me in THE SHADOW.
Heaven will have to make room for this little
bateau.

'By the way, I hope to live to a hundred
or so'.

MY SUNGLASSES

My sunglasses are simply out of sight.
Do you know what? I put them on at night.

60

INDEX OF FIRST LINES

A NOISY NOISE ANNOYS

Compiled by JENNIFER CURRY
Illustrated by SUSIE JENKIN-PEARCE

*Bursting with poetic talent from Brian
Patten and William Shakespeare to
Thomas Hardy and Wes Magee, A NOISY
NOISE ANNOYS will take you on an aural
adventure of awesome proportions!
Sounds good? Great! Now read on...*

No nerve was left unjangled
When Nicola learnt the fiddle.
She scraped it high
She scraped it low
She scraped it in the middle.

Mike Jubb

RED FOX paperback, £3.50 ISBN 0 09 952801 0
THE BODLEY HEAD hardback, £9.99 ISBN 0 370 32301 7

Bumwigs and Earbeetles
and other Unspeakable Delights

Poems by ANN ZIETY
Illustrated by LESLEY BISSEKER

*Think ghastly! Think grisly! Think grim!
BUMWIGS AND EARBEETLES is all those
things... and worse!!!
Smelly socks, crumbly compost heaps and mangy
moggies are among the unthinkable, unspeakable
delights in this collection.*

Catch a whiff of this...

MY DOG NEVER HAD FLEAS
he had bumwigs and earbeetles
and sinus larvae
and one or two exaggerated boils
and bits of ticks that stuck to his ears
and sticky mites
and bites from fights
and stashes and stashes of nasty rashes
but he never had fleas
not one

Coming soon!
RED FOX paperback, £3.50 ISBN 0 09 953961 6
Out now!
BODLEY HEAD hardback, £8.99 ISBN 0 370 31975 3

Sold in aid of
the Malcolm Sargent
Cancer Fund for
Children

I REMEMBER, I REMEMBER

*Famous People's Favourite
Childhood Poems*

Compiled by ROB FARROW
Illustrated by TREVOR NEWTON

*Dip into these memorable poems, picked by a
dazzling array of celebrities. Find out why
they've chosen each poem – or in Gazza's case,
how he became a poet for the day...*

JUST ME by Paul Gascoigne

I'm a professional footballer
lying in a hospital bed
thinking of all those nasty things
all going through my head

I know I should not be lying here
it's because of Wembley
thinking of that stupid tackle...

*Ooops! Sorry, you'll have to net a copy of the book if
you want to find out what happens next!*

I REMEMBER, I REMEMBER
RED FOX paperback, £3.50 ISBN 0 09 931831 8